THAMES

RODNEY PIER

WATERLOO BRIDGE

T0158336

ROYAL
FESTIVAL
HALL

20

19

27

WATERLOO
BRIDGE GATE

17

18

23

24

SOUTH BANK EXHIBITION

21 Sport

22 Seaside

23 Television

24 Telecinema

25 1851 Centenary Pavilion

26 Shot Tower

27 Design Review

RESTAURANTS

A The Rocket

B Fairway Cafe

C The Dairy Bar

D The Whistle

E The '51'

F The Skylark

G Regatta Restaurant

H The Turntable Cafe

I The Unicorn

J The Garden Cafe

K Thameside Restaurant

L Harbour Bar

M Royal Festival Hall

Paul Rennie

Festival of Britain

1951

Antique Collectors' Club

Design format by Webb & Webb Design Limited, London

The images used in this book come mainly from the Collection of
Paul and Karen Rennie. The Publishers would also like to thank and
acknowledge the following for permission to use their images:

The Royal Festival Hall Archives for images of the Royal Festival
Hall, past and present, on pages 6-7

The Estate of Edward Bawden for The British Character and
Tradition Festival Screen on page 46

London's Transport Museum (www.ltmuseum.co.uk) and the Estate
of Abram Games (www.abramgames.com) for use of the London
Transport poster on page 95

The Estate of Abram Games for use of the Games Festival logo

Every effort has been made to secure the relevant permission to
reproduce the images contained within this book. Any errors or
omissions are unintentional and details should be addressed to the
publisher.

ISBN: 978-1-85149-533-7

British Library Cataloguing-in-Publication Data.
A catalogue record for this book is available from the British Library.

Antique Collectors' Club
www.antiquecollectorsclub.com

Sandy Lane, Old Martlesham, Woodbridge, Suffolk IP12 4SD, UK
T: 01394 389950 F: 01394 389999
E: info@antique-acc.com
or
ACC Distribution
6 West 18th Street, Suite 4B, New York, NY 10011, USA
T: 212 645 1111 F: 212 989 3205
E: sales@antiquecc.com

Published by Antique Collectors' Club, Woodbridge, England
Printed and bound in China

Plan now to visit the

FESTIVAL

OF BRITAIN

May–September 1951

1951 is Festival year in Britain ! *Festival of Britain* year, when, for five eventful months—from May to September—all Britain will be on show ! For the 1951 Festival is being staged on a *nationwide* basis— in London and at centres throughout the country. It will present for your enjoyment a fascinating programme of exhibitions and musical and dramatic events, demonstrating Britain's achievements in the arts, science and industry. Festival year will be a great year to ' Come to Britain '. Plan your trip now. See your travel agent for further, fuller details; or write to the 1951 Festival Information Centre, 47 Leicester Square, London, W.C.2, England ; or The British Travel Centre, 336 Madison Avenue, N.Y., U.S.A.   *Programme of Events overleaf.*

Typographic flyer showing the use of decorated, italicised and 'fat' display type as an expression of the Festival style

Festival matchbook

CONTENTS

FOREWORD

Not long after arriving from Australia to take up my role as Chief Executive of the Southbank Centre, I chanced upon a delightful shop just off Lambs Conduit Street in Bloomsbury, my new local patch. I then had the pleasure of meeting the owner, Paul Rennie, and discussing his obsession with the Festival of Britain 1951, in particular the extraordinary design legacy the Festival has had on modern Britain.

I bought my first piece of Festival of Britain memorabilia and became fascinated by the event itself and its enduring impact on British design, largely thanks to Paul and to my role in leading Royal Festival Hall into the 21st Century.

When Jude Kelly was appointed as our Artistic Director, she deepened my interest in the Festival. She infused us all with the knowledge of the event itself and inspired us to think about how in our plans to transform the Royal Festival Hall we could pay tribute to the extraordinary things that had happened on the site, the contributions by the thousands of artists, many of them refugees from the hideousness of the War, and to the sheer sense of fun and joy that the Festival created for millions of Britons.

We are reopening the Royal Festival Hall in a way that celebrates the legacy of the Festival of Britain in 1951, but also makes important statements about the arts, design and the access by all people to these grand institutions today and into the future.

We hope that in our labours we shall do justice to the work that Paul Rennie has championed for many years – through his academic work and his collecting. Our aim is to rightfully give credit to the enormous legacy of the Festival as we move into the second life of the Festival's only architectural survivor: Royal Festival Hall.

I shall treasure my brass Festival plaque for many years as I remember Paul Rennie's wonderful shop in Bloomsbury and my great memories of the Hall and this wonderful site in this most fantastic of cities.

May the legacy live on!

Michael Lynch AM
Chief Executive, Southbank Centre
2007

Official Guide to the South Bank exhibit of the Festival, with emblem and geometric design by Abram Games

INTRODUCTION

The Festival of Britain took place between May and September of 1951. It was conceived as an event to commemorate the centenary of The Great Exhibition of 1851 and to celebrate the history, achievements and potential of the Britain people. Furthermore, the timing of the Festival would, it was hoped, mark the end of austerity and begin a programme of democratic engagement with art, science and technology. The Festival was a practical expression of the ideas shaping reconstruction after WWII. At the same time, the Festival was offered as a moment of light relief, a kind of national village fete, and promoted as 'A Tonic to the Nation'.

This little book examines the objects, souvenirs and printed ephemera produced to commemorate the Festival of Britain in 1951, providing an introduction and guide for students and collectors.

The material presented here, however modest, is significant historical evidence in its own right. The popular history to which these objects attest is, for various reasons, continuously revised and this evidence may, in consequence, provide a counter-argument. Accordingly, this material is of interest to a wide variety of students at various levels, in terms of both social history and in relation to design. Indeed, its special value is that, unlike the iconic objects preferred by design history, these objects provide an insight to the popular taste of 1951. One of the purposes of this book is to help you construct your own archive and historical interpretation of the Festival; a bibliography is included as a further help.

The souvenir objects of the Festival were, due to the nature of the Festival, ephemeral keepsakes that were both mementos and, at the same time, celebrations of the future. We might now consider them as a kind of 'archaeology' of the future: because where we are now is different from where we expected to be, back in 1951, these objects offer a glimpse into an alternative world with its attendant possibility of a different and parallel future. Although, of course, this type of imaginative engagement is commonplace in relation to literary experience, our response to the objects and ephemera of recent popular culture is generally more prosaic.

My interest in the Festival was an accident of birth: my father was ordered, as part of his National Service, to help at the South Bank. The Royal Engineers laid a Bailey bridge, made up of modular and prefabricated units, across the Thames just next to Hungerford Bridge. Later, my father worked as an architect in the offices of Coventry City Council.

I can just about remember the excitement and pride of Coventry as it recast itself as an exemplar of post-war reconstruction and social democracy. Of course, the relief and idealism that drove those feelings were obscure to me. Nor could I know how these feelings related to the terrible experiences of November 1940. But I did feel part of something bigger than my immediate family and recognised it as exciting, impressive and good.

Those early memories stayed with me. Later, in the mid-1970s, through a developing interest in things, I became aware that the progressive idealism of post-war reconstruction was contested. I was conscious of a debate in which Modernism, the post-war consensus, and the status of Britain were all called into question.

My reaction to this was practical. I began to collect objects and works of art associated with British Modernism. The Festival had always been familiar to me: my father's snap-shots of the South Bank dominated the early pages of our family photo album. It was natural, since I already knew about the Festival, to begin by collecting objects and souvenirs associated with 1951.

In 1980 these objects were unregarded and inexpensive. It was a great adventure to go out with Karen, my future wife, and search for these little treasures at Camden Lock or wherever. Ironically, one of the first objects we bought turned out to be quite rare. I was lucky enough to be able to purchase the black-and-white Festival mug designed by Norman Makinson for Wedgwood. This had been left over from a pioneering show of 20th-century ceramics at Richard Dennis. The mug exists in two versions: one coloured and the other plain. This object was obviously aimed at the quality end of the market and relatively few were sold; it is surprising how small Wedgwood's production of these souvenirs was.

My enjoyment of the Festival has always been, to some extent, vicarious. I was unable to visit the Festival and it exists, for me at least, as an interpretation of objects and folk-memory. I always begin with the objects and, through looking at them, try and discern a cultural background of ideas, technology and design. Here, my interests are in design history, the political economy of Britain's souvenir culture and the relationship, expressed as memory, between people and objects.

Over the years Karen and I have kept collecting and the project has grown. Now we have collections of graphic design, textiles and objects as well as a large box of Festival souvenirs. It is a pleasure to share some of these alongside a few additions from friends and colleagues.

The visual presentation of this selection is determined, in part at least, by the strengths and weaknesses of the collection. The souvenir glassware and Festival compacts are noticeable by their absence, for which I apologise.

Souvenir in Pictures Guide published by the *News Chronicle*

THE FESTIVAL OF BRITAIN 1951

Political Organisation

The political origins of the Festival are quite straightforward. The first proposal for a post-war and celebratory festival was made at a meeting of the Royal Society of Arts, London, in 1943. The proposal suggested a centenary commemoration of the Great Exhibition of 1851 as a suitable pretext.[1]

Gerald Barry, editor of the *News Chronicle*, took up the idea in an open letter to Sir Stafford Cripps, President of the Board of Trade in 1945. Barry's first proposal was for an international event styled on the traditional trade fair. A government committee under the chairmanship of Lord Ramsden discussed this possibility at some length before deciding against it on grounds of cost.

At this point the Board of Trade, judging themselves to be a forward-looking and internationalist body dedicated to developing trade, declined any strategic role in the Festival.

Lord Ramsden made it clear, however, that a national exhibition of the type originally suggested remained possible. The deputy Prime Minister, Herbert Morrison took up the proposal and began to promote the idea of "a national festival that displayed the British contribution to civilisation, past, present and future, in the arts science and industrial design".

The idea was presented formally to the House of Commons on the 7th December 1947. The proposal received cross-party support and the Festival was granted a budget of £12 million.

Morrison's main job in 1947 was as an organiser of economic

planning. It is possible that Morrison seized on the Festival project as, in contrast to his mainly administrative duties, it might provide a tangible achievement within a relatively short period of time.

Complex problems, caused by external events, consistently strained budgets and materials. The years preceding the Festival had been difficult ones. There were sterling crises at regular intervals and the economics of devaluation played themselves out through shortages of the most basic commodities in construction: labour and materials.

Morrison began the planning of the Festival by appointing Gerald Barry as its director. Barry's journalistic and public relations expertise helped keep the Festival story in the news throughout the difficult period of its genesis. The popularity of the Festival, when it opened, was a tribute to his effort.

Morrison also authorised the appointment of staff to a Festival office that became a government department. Morrison then went on to select a Festival Council to support and guide the director in his duties, in part to assure the project some political independence. The Council formed an advisory body made up of establishment figures, including a number of politicians, representative of different parts of the country, and experts on the broad themes of the Festival: Sir Malcom Sargent for music, Sir Robert Robinson for science, John Gielgud and Noel Coward for the stage, Sir Kenneth Clark for the fine arts and Sir Ernest Pooley representing the Arts Council. The presence of two Conservatives of considerable standing on the Council, during a time of Labour government, further enhanced the Council's role in demonstrating that the Festival was non-partisan in party political terms.

Morrison chose Lord Ismay as chairman of the Festival Council. Ismay had been Churchill's Chief Staff Officer during The Second World War and had played an important part in the negotiations for Indian independence. Ismay was a very senior figure and enjoyed a close friendship with Churchill. His appointment may be regarded as an exemplary piece of political manoeuvring to forward the Festival project.

Ismay later recalled that he agreed to accept the chairmanship because, although an "ignoramus in science and somewhat a Philistine about the arts", he was frightened the government would send him abroad again if he refused it. Whatever, the fact remains that Ismay did a very effective job in persuading everyone to work together as a team.

The Council held its first meeting on 31 May 1948. Eight days later Ismay and Barry held a Festival briefing, at London's Guildhall, with the leaders of all the local government authorities. They explained that, although the centrepiece of the Festival would be in London, they wanted the celebrations to extend across every part of the country. The government would be paying for two travelling exhibitions, however, there was no other budget available for local events. Therefore, Ismay concluded, the success of the Festival, at a national level, would depend "on the spontaneous co-operation of civic authorities throughout the British Isles".

The response of the local authorities to Ismay's appeal was impressive. As Ismay later recalled in his memoirs, the meeting "lit a flame that spread like a prairie fire" through every part of the country: Glasgow organised an industrial exhibition; Belfast put on a factories exhibition; the Arts Council sponsored twenty-two arts festivals; and over 2,000 places organised some form of Festival celebration.

The choice of a main site for the Festival was soon made. There was an area of bomb-damaged land between Waterloo Bridge and County Hall, on London's South Bank. The site had one important advantage: it was central and close to Waterloo. This proximity to central London assured immediate and convenient transport links to the Festival. In addition, the widespread use of electric trains from Waterloo greatly reduced the blight of smoke and soot usually associated with railways. This enhanced the potential of the open spaces at the South Bank. The riverside promenade could, in consequence, become a central feature of the Festival site.

The only disadvantage of the site was the limited access from the north bank of the Thames. This problem was solved by the creation of a Festival Gateway in Northumberland Avenue and a direct access to the site across a Bailey bridge.

The Festival opened, on time, on 3 May 1951. This was almost exactly three years to the day after the first Council meeting. The opening ceremonies began with Their Majesties King George VI and Queen Elizabeth driving in state to St Paul's cathedral for a service attended by a congregation of 3,000. From the steps of St Paul's, The King then declared the Festival open. In his speech, broadcast to the nation, The King explained that Britain had recently suffered the grievous losses of two World Wars and that though it had made some steps toward recovery the country now found itself facing new burdens at time of international uncertainty. The King remained optimistic of Britain's abiding courage and vitality as displayed through the Festival.[2]

Over the next five months more than 8½ million people visited the Festival site on the South Bank. Many people also attended the variety of independently-arranged local events. Ismay mentions in his memoirs visiting music festivals in Canterbury, York and Swansea, a 'Regency' historic festival in Brighton, a 'Farm and Factory' exhibition in Belfast, a festival of ancient crafts and traditions in Chipping Camden, and an exhibition of industries in Bristol. The number of people who visited these attractions is unknown.

Morrison made the Festival a success. He refused to consider the Festival as a party political project and successfully championed it as a national enterprise. His commitment to the Festival ensured that the scheme, when it was finally realised, bore an obvious similarity to the scale and scope of the enterprise originally proposed. There were, inevitably, political criticisms about this expense at a time of austerity and, perhaps, of more urgent priorities. Morrison responded to all criticism by reminding these political critics that the Festival had been agreed to by all parties. In the event, the immediate and enormous popular success of the Festival unequivocally answered these critics.

The ceremony marking the end of the Festival, on 30 September 1951, consisted of a short service and the massed bands of the Brigade of Guards beating the Retreat and Tattoo.

Looking back, Ismay felt that the Festival helped generate a feeling of unity and a sense that, after two devastating World Wars, the British people were determined to move on.

Cover design for RIBA architectural and planning proposals *Towards a New Britain*, 1945. Note the optimistic parasol, flat roofs and vaulted arcades

Photograph of the South Bank looking west towards the Dome of Discovery

Design Management

The design of the Festival was delegated to the Design Group under Hugh Casson. Casson's most important colleagues in the Design Group were James Holland and James Gardner. The Festival Pattern Group and the Typographic Panel supported the Design Group through a co-ordinating role across the various Festival sites. Casson, as the senior figure, acted as a bridge between the architects and planners and the political figures steering the Festival project.

The choice of Hugh Casson to head the Design Group has been the subject of much discussion. On the one hand, Casson was revealed as an accomplished architectural fixer. Manser tells the story in some detail.[3] Casson was able to match projects and personalities and to assure an overall visual coherence to the

Festival so as best to communicate the progressive humanist values at the heart of the project. On the other hand and to his critics, Casson attached the Festival to a set of pre-war architectural objectives that undermined the progressive potential of its design.

The buildings, exhibits and planning of the South Bank were conceived to provide a vivid template for the reconstruction of Britain. The whole was a Modernist architectural expression of materials, technology and engineering. The austere utilitarian provisions of WWII were replaced by a sophisticated integration of art, design and architecture.

The South Bank also boasted state-of-the-art public conveniences and was credited with introducing luxury toilet paper to ordinary people. Whether this Festival paper was marked with the official emblem has not been recorded.

Modern architecture, in its most logically coherent form, eschewed all forms of decoration in favour of functional utility and material integrity. The resulting autonomy of architecture, in relation to the other arts, became the default for aspiring radicals working in other fields. In consequence, the attempt to integrate art and architecture became more a process of positioning one in relation to the other. The difficulty of creating a coherently Modernist and, at the same time, festive experience across the South Bank became the major problem facing the Design Group.

Casson and his colleagues solved this problem by exploiting a special feature of the site they had been given. One of the most appealing characteristics of the South Bank site was the chance it gave to promenade along the Thames and between buildings. The idea of promenading was taken from the holiday spirit of the English seaside and of the earlier entertainments at Vauxhall Gardens and elsewhere. The psychological benefits of this access-all-areas approach should not be underestimated. It marked a crucial change from the security-inspired restrictions on movement imposed during WWII.

The decision to turn the South Bank into a promenade was far more radical than it seems. In 1951 it was not obvious that promenading by the riverside was the attractive proposition that it has become fifty years later. At the time, the river was still an industrial highway with levels of traffic were far beyond what we see today. The air quality in London remained poor (in 1952 the smog killed over 4000 people) and called into question the kinds of outdoor leisure activities promoted as a continental-style cafe-culture. The promotion of a democratic Thames-side promenade must have seemed almost unimaginably sophisticated in 1951.

The visual identity of a reclaimed South Bank was first given expression by Gordon Cullen in the Architectural Review during 1949. Cullen was an architectural draughtsman of rare skill. His sense of texture and his eye for detail identified him as a Modernist. However, he retained a sensitivity for the quirky, the historical and the home-made. The result was a unique visualisation of the potential contained within urban environments. Later, in 1961, Cullen articulated these observations more fully in his theory of *Townscape*.

Under Casson's direction, the Festival encouraged the development of an architectural style that was both substantial and light-hearted. The exemplars of seaside and village fête were discreetly on hand throughout. One example of this can be found in the use of bunting throughout the site and on the Festival emblem.

The design of one of the most remarkable features of the Festival, the Skylon, also illustrates the sense of intelligent gaiety that Casson and the Design Group were intent on promoting. Quite apart from its ingenuity, the Skylon was a reminder of the exciting sculptural potential of an architectural *jeu d'esprit*.

The temporary nature of the Festival also helps to explain Casson's approach to its buildings. The Design Group knew that all the buildings on the South Bank Site, with the exception of the Festival Hall, would be demolished after five months. It was sensible, therefore, to think of the buildings as temporary pavilions.

The building and exhibits were positioned around the South Bank to encourage the visitors to make the best use of it. The exhibits, laid out in the various pavilions and buildings were organised into two separate, but inter-woven narratives: *People* and *Land*. These were conceived, in part at least, to divide the large number of visitors into two, more manageable, streams. The two circuits were identified as Upstream and Downstream.

These narratives form the basis of Ian Cox's various official guides to the Festival sites, especially his *Guide to the South Bank Exhibition and the Story it Tells*, and its sister publication the *Catalogue of Exhibits*. The latter document provides a comprehensive and detailed list of all the objects and works of art exhibited on the South Bank. Barry Curtis has carefully itemised the narrative unity of this organisation of material.[4]

However, the Design Group was not only interested in encouraging visitors to move around the site in an orderly way: Casson and his colleagues organised the South Bank into spaces between buildings, where visitors were encouraged to sit, relax and enjoy a show. The show included the buildings, the art works and other visitors. By night, the South Bank and the Pleasure Gardens at Battersea became popular for fireworks, open-air dancing and riverside dining. The relative sophistication of these entertainments, for ordinary people and in the context of post-war austerity, should not be discounted.

From Casson's point-of-view, the Festival was an important success and helped to make him the Establishment's 'safe-pair-of-hands' in relation to managing design projects. He continued with this managerial role at the Royal College of Art and then at the Royal Academy of Arts.

The Festival Emblem

The Festival emblem was the product of a design competition organised by the Arts Council and the Council for Industrial Design. The Festival Office requested submissions from twelve specially-selected designers, representing both the established names of British commercial art along as well as some of the younger personalities of design. Among those chosen for inclusion were Reynolds Stone, Milner Gray, Richard Guyatt and Lynton Lamb from the old guard. Amongst the newer names were Abram Games, Tom Eckersley, FHK Henrion and Robin Day.

The competition brief set out the requirements for a symbol that could be applied universally to products and documents. The symbol was to be used officially by the Festival authorities and was also to be allowed as a mark of approval on a range of non-official products. The brief suggested that the symbol must be suitable for effective use on letter headings, tickets, posters and badges and also, in larger scale, as architectural detail. In addition, the successful symbol would communicate something of "a summer of gaiety and good looks".[5]

Finding a suitable symbol for the Festival was a complex problem. The cast of possibilities for something recognisable and appealing, across the whole nation, was relatively constrained. Many of those possibilities had been over used during WWII and, as a consequence, even in 1951, carried with them a trace of martial propaganda.

The winning design, by Abram Games, presented Britannia, in profile, above a four-pointed star representing the points of a compass, to illustrate the truly national aspect of the Festival. A festive spirit was incorporated into the design through the addition of a swag of red and blue bunting that enclosed the date, 1951.

The successful design for the Festival emblem established Abram Games as the most significant graphic artist of his generation. In

International poster for BOAC services to the Festival with
emblem by Abram Games and Festival titling

fact, Games deserves to be counted amongst the most important graphic artists of the 20th century.

Abram Games is best known for his work during WWII. Games had revealed himself, in his capacity as poster designer to the War Office, to be a master of graphic communication. The circumstances of national emergency and the urgent moral claims implicit in the war-effort were ideally suited to his idealistic nature. The Festival brief allowed Games to express his social idealism in altogether more benign circumstances.

Games described his design methodology as working towards "maximum meaning through minimum means". The striving towards simplicity and economy that this implied can be seen in the working drawings that Games produced as part of the process of refining his idea. The progressives for his Festival design are reproduced as the endpapers for his monograph.[6]

The Festival marked a high-water-mark in peacetime poster design for Abram Games. The success of the Festival emblem was matched by that of his *Financial Times* poster, which began a series of commissions lasting throughout the decade. Looking back, the Festival emblem and those posters define the graphic style of the decade perfectly.[7]

Abram Games was always fiercely protective of the commercial value and intellectual property of his designs. However, the Festival emblem was uniquely and from the first, made freely available to official and unofficial users alike. The relative simplicity of the Festival emblem made it ideally suited, as the brief had intended, for use on any surface and in every size. Quite apart from its commercial uses, the emblem also proved highly popular with the organisers beyond the South Bank.

Abram Games was always especially proud of the popular success of his Festival design and he took special pleasure in his collection of the various interpretations given to his emblem.

Metal, enamel, painted and plastic badges with emblem

The South Bank

The main site of the Festival was on the south bank of the Thames in London. Before 1951, the site, opposite Whitehall and the Strand, was dominated by the presence of Waterloo Station on its southern edge and by the Hungerford railway and Waterloo bridges. To the west, the site was bordered by County Hall and Westminster Bridge. At its eastern extremity, downstream, the site was bordered by Waterloo Road and marked by the Shot Tower. The old Lion brewery, whose classical frontage was embellished by the figure of the South Bank Lion, stood prominently on the riverside. (The lion, made of Coade's Artificial Stone, now stands on the southern side of Westminster Bridge.) Of course, most noticeable of all was the expansive sweep of the Thames.

Until relatively recently the Surrey side of the Thames has existed in sharp architectural, social and cultural contrast to the northern Middlesex side. Nowhere was this contrast greater than in central London. On the northern side were the buildings associated with

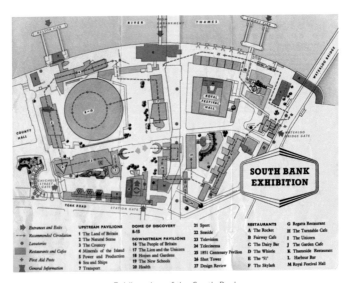

Folding plan of the South Bank

A sheet of gummed souvenir 'Cinderella' stamps

the execution of political power, influence and prestige. The architectural style of the buildings reflected these concerns and the whole had been organised into a plan with wide avenues so as to effectively communicate Britain's Imperial destiny. In contrast, the south bank remained a densely packed area of wharfs, warehouses, tenements and slums, to which most Londoners did not venture.

The Design Group recognised that the most dramatic view of the Festival's South Bank was from across the river. Unfortunately, both Westminster and Waterloo bridges were at either extremity of the site and gave only a partial view. In order to bring visitors directly to the heart of the South Bank site, a Bailey bridge was erected in the lee of Hungerford Bridge.[8] At its northern end the bridge was accessible from Northumberland Avenue.

The approach to the bridge was illuminated with large Festival Star lights above the street. The bridge itself was decked with bunting and provided an exciting portal to the site. By the time visitors had reached the South Bank, they were in high spirits. From the Bailey bridge approach all the main building of the South Bank were visible.

The Main Structures

The Festival Hall

The centrepiece of the South Bank was the Festival Hall. This concert venue was conceived as a replacement venue for the Queen's Hall. Its scale and the obvious permanence of its design and execution allowed it to dominate the whole site. The architects for the Hall were the London County Council's team led by Leslie Martin, Robert Matthew and Peter Moro.[9]

The Festival Hall was the first major public building to be completed in London since before the WWII. Its completion was therefore symbolic of a renewed commitment to the cultural life of the capital. This committment was further emphasised by some of the technical and functional characteristics of the new building. The acoustic quality of the hall and the comfort of the audience were prioritised, providing a state-of-the-art venue. In fact, the impression given by the arrangement of elements and their specifications was entirely positive: there were no poor seats in the auditorium, the structure allowed for clear sight lines to the stage from every part of the hall. The implication of this, particularly in relation to the Royal Box, was obviously egalitarian.

The second characteristic of the hall was the absence of crushed interval areas around the approaches and exits to the auditorium. By placing the main concert space in the centre of the building and surrounding it on all sides with public spaces the architects achieved two objectives: the size of the hall was the maximum possible for the footprint of the site and the size of the audience was easily accommodated by the relative spaciousness of the supporting areas around the building.

These spaces were an instant success and the Festival Hall quickly became a social meeting place as much as a concert venue. The foyer areas, arranged on levels that matched the raked seating of the auditorium, provided interestingly varied social spaces with a wide range of perspectives. The large windows and balcony

View of the Festival Hall from across the river,
drawn by Gordon Cullen

Elevated walkways surrounding the Festival Hall

Festival Guide

Guide to Battersea Pleasure Gardens,
cover by Hans Tisdall

Special issue *Sight and Sound* magazine

Festival of Britain Guide – Lambeth Edition

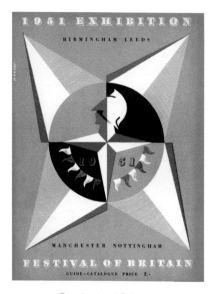

Travelling Land Exhibition

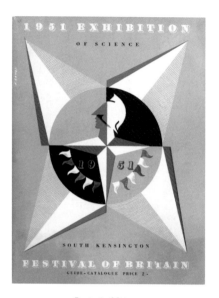

Festival of Science

Festival Ship Campania

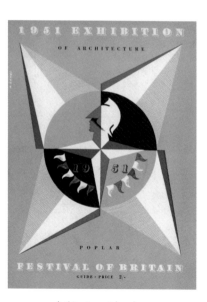

Architecture at Lansbury

platforms further enhanced the general feeling of comfortable openness. The pleasing ambiguities of inside and outside were made possible by the whole structure being supported principally by the steel frame enclosing the auditorium. The widespread use of large-scale plants within the interior again distinguished this space as both modern and comfortable.

The Festival Hall exemplified the rational, democratic and Utopian ideals of the Festival and earned its title of 'The People's Palace'.

The Dome of Discovery

The largest building on the South Bank was the Dome of Discovery. This flat, flying saucer shaped structure presented a narrative of scientific exploration across various scientific and environmental contexts. Together, these displays accounted for about half of the upstream *Land* circuit of the Festival.[10] The Dome was situated at the upstream extremity of the South Bank.

Ralph Tubbs designed the Dome as a series of concrete platforms on different levels all covered with a single span. The roof of the Dome was an aluminium structure made out of a triangulated lattice covered with a lightweight skin. The Dome was the largest of its kind as well as being the biggest aluminium structure ever built. The Dome successfully anticipated the geodesic megastructures of Buckminster Fuller and Cedric Price.

The most spectacular characteristics of the Dome were its scale and the polished roof surface. The machine aesthetic implied by the structure was an obvious expression of the scientific intelligence displayed within.

The exterior of the Dome was so arranged as to provide a canopied area of shelter. These were furnished with the special chairs designed for the Festival by Ernest Race and by Robin Day. After beginning his career in graphic design, Robin Day later specialised in furniture design where he worked in partnership with the manufacturers Hille. Ernest Race remains less well know, his *Antelope* chair, designed as outdoor furniture for the Festival, exemplifies the 1950s style in Britain.

The Skylon

The great horizontal sweep of the Dome was placed in contrast to an altogether more ambiguous structure: the Skylon. This was a piece of architectural sculpture created as a vertical feature on the riverfront of the South Bank, and cleverly designed to have no visible means of support.

The structure was designed by Powell and Moya as a lightweight and illuminated aluminium element held in tensioned suspension by a series of triangulated steel ropes and poles. The origins of the Skylon were to be found in the association of a historic nautical tradition and the more recent materials and calculus of airframe engineering. The result was something new, surprising and delightful.

The Skylon was possibly the most popular and fondly-remembered element of the South Bank. With hindsight, the Skylon has been recognised as an architectural statement of panache and style that anticipated the later interest by architects and engineers in tensioned structures. Accordingly, the Millennium Dome may be seen as a 21st-century attempt to combine elements of tension, structure and scale that were first seen on the Festival's South Bank in 1951.

Sea and Ships Pavilion

Adjacent to the Skylon, and facing the river, was the Sea and Ships Pavilion designed by Basil Spence. This was a particularly difficult brief as the structure had to accommodate some very large exhibits. Spence created a dramatic arrangement of elevated walkways around these focal points.

Spence was subsequently awarded the commission for Coventry Cathedral that established him as a stellar name in the immediate post-war architectural scene. His integration of art and architecture in a more permanent and refined setting is recognised as an enduring and popular archetype of English Modernism.

The work at Coventry also began a series of collaborations between architects and engineers, principally Ted Happold and Peter Rice at Ove Arup's *Special Structures Group*, that helped define the trajectory of late 20th century architecture through its association with a series of revolutionary structures around the world.

The Shot Tower

A second vertical element was made from the old Shot Tower at the downstream end of the site, with Hugh Casson responsible for its transformation. Built in 1826, the tower was the oldest surviving structure on the South Bank. Originally conceived, as its name implies, for making lead shot, the tower was crowned with a series of tele-communication aerials mounted on an old anti-aircraft gun platform.

The Shot Tower was owned by Associated Lead, a manufacturer of lead and antimony products, who moved production to Chester to accommodate the Festival. The Tower was later demolished for redevelopment.[11]

The Lion and the Unicorn Pavillion

Another part of the Festival story was presented through the Lion and Unicorn Pavillion. The exhibits shown here were laid out so as to express the defining qualities of the British people.

Defining the national character is notoriously difficult: designers of this exhibit chose the lion and unicorn as symbols of contrasting aspects of the national character. No doubt there was a subliminal reference to George Orwell's wartime polemic that had used the same references to underpin his call for political revolution and social transformation in Britain.

In 1951, the lion was used to symbolise courage and fortitude. The unicorn, on the other hand, was used to express the eccentricity and good humour that are understood as characteristic of British social tolerance and political freedom.[12]

The exhibition was designed around the idea that the English language, with its expressive potential and in all its regional variations, was linked to the historical development of romanticism, eccentricity and inventiveness. Each of these characteristics was, for the purposes of the exhibition, identified as essential to national identity. The writer Laurie Lee wrote the captions for the exhibit. John Lewis and John Brinkley, typographers at Cowell's of Ipswich, designed the typography for this display.[13]

The whole was conceived as a counterpoint to the unrelenting rationalist didacticism implicit in the surrounding scientific and technical exhibits across the South Bank.

It was natural, given the brief, that the Lion and Unicorn Pavilion should explore aspects of British history. In addition to the usual historical narratives of power and money, the exhibit explored more whimsical themes. The choice of peculiar and fantastic objects drawn from the popular traditions of folk memory and rural life expressed an alternative evolution of national character.

The whimsical characteristic of the Festival story was further embellished in an exhibition of folk art at London's Whitechapel art gallery. The exhibition was organised by Barbara Jones and entitled *Black Eyes and Lemonade*. Barbara Jones was a gifted architectural watercolourist who had worked on the *Architectural Review* and as a member of the *Recording Britain* scheme during WWII.

The exhibition was planned to provide a social and historical context, illustrated through objects, for the neo-romantic and surrealist tendencies of modern artists in Britain. This conceptually ambitious scheme sought to reconcile nostalgia with more utopian and imaginative musings. The ambiguous title for the exhibit is from a line by the Irish poet Thomas Moore (1813)

> *A Persian's heaven is easily made:*
> *_'Tis but black eyes and lemonade.*

Jigsaw of the Emett Light Railway, Battersea

Beyond the South Bank

Beyond the South Bank there were important, official, elements of the Festival at Lansbury, in London's East End, on the Festival Ship *Campania* and at Battersea.

Lansbury

The London Blitz of 1940 and 1941 established an unofficial political agenda where military objectives and social transformation were combined. The first expressions of this unexpected alignment were published by *Picture Post* in their 'Plan for Britain'[14] and by George Orwell.[15] The full extent of the war damage to London's infrastructure and housing stock made reconstruction an urgent priority. The publication of Abercrombie's *Greater London Plan*[16] established a framework where issues of reconstruction and social progress combined in the utopian idealism of slum clearance, New Town development and green belt conservation. Broadly speaking, the Festival acknowledged these aims and gave expression to the idealism of social transformation through design, planning and architecture.

The Festival offered an ideal opportunity to showcase this policy. The construction of the Lansbury Estate in the London Borough of Poplar, became a kind of living laboratory for the study of reconstruction and regeneration. The architectural exhibit at Lansbury, whilst obviously a work-in-progress, provided a practical demonstration of how the utopian ideals of reconstruction could help resolve the problems associated with traffic congestion, depressed housing, inadequate open space and the intermingling of industry and housing.[17]

The *Guide to Lansbury* explains how materials, functional considerations and community combine to provide an architectural space centred on new housing stock, market place, primary schools and places of worship. Even the public house is recast as a contemporary structure. The Lansbury Estate covers an area of over three square miles.

It is immediately obvious that the townscape model of Lansbury provided a sort of modernist version of more recent architectural initiatives in residential regeneration. The development achieved high densities without recourse to high-rise or system building. The prioritisation of people and community over traffic and commerce is in sharp contrast to the kinds of urban schemes that promote the relentless pursuit of consumption in retail leisure environments.

Travelling Land Exhibit and Festival Ship *Campania*

The Festival was conceived as a "constellation of events" uniting the people of Britain and celebrating their achievements. It was natural, in these circumstances, for the organisers of the Festival to want to reach beyond the London metropolis.

Two major parts of this strategy were the Land Travelling Exhibition and the Festival Ship *Campania*. The Land exhibit travelled to Birmingham, Leeds, Manchester and Leeds, whilst *Campania* visited Southampton, Dundee, Newcastle, Hull, Plymouth, Bristol, Cardiff, Belfast, Birkenhead and Glasgow.

There were also exhibitions of Science at South Kensington, Industrial Power in Glasgow and Farm and Factory in Northern

Ireland. To a large extent these other exhibits were intended to give a summary of the main narratives presented at the South Bank. A multitude of smaller, more local, exhibitions and events presented their communities as part of this Festival constellation. Each of these events is commemorated by a pamphlet, catalogue, badge or object, so the potential for assembling a widely diverse collection of official and unofficial souvenirs is enormous.

Battersea Pleasure Gardens

The Festival was not relentlessly educational. At the South Bank there was evening dining and dancing beneath the moonlight. Further upstream, at Battersea, a pleasure garden was laid out to provide a relaxed and enjoyable counterpoint to the main Festival experience.

In the *Pleasure Garden's Guide*, A.P. Herbert[18] writes

> *Welcome to the World! To London's Garden Fair,*
> *Where Britain, modestly, lets down her hair.*
> *You've seen beside the shores of Waterloo,*
> *What solemn things the local natives do.*
> *Here, in our quaint, unconventional way,*
> *We aim at beauty and pursue the gay.*

Here was an area devoted to entertainments, enjoyments and pleasure. The Garden was proposed as a continuation of the Festival experience. It was assumed, therefore, that visitors would begin to arrive later in the day and special boats were provided to ferry visitors upstream from Waterloo to Chelsea.

The Gardens were laid out so as to provide a Terrace Walk, Parade and Fun Fair. Passages of formal planting were contrasted with more eccentric elements. In the evening the lanterns, flood lighting and water displays evoked the historical gardens of Vauxhall, Cremorne and Ranelagh.

The flavours of Battersea were, in contrast to those of the South Bank, exotic and eccentric. The architecture of the Gardens included various fantasies such as a pagoda and pavilion. These exotic, Oriental structures implicitly refer to a set of values defined as a counterpoint to those prevailing at home.

Two of the major attractions at Battersea were the *Guinness Clock* designed by Lewitt Him, and *The Far Tottering and Oyster Creek Railway* designed by Rowland Emett. These whimsical inventions expressed another side of the British character.

The combinations of ornament, lighting and movement, set amidst the picturesque provide something at once familiar and exotic. In contrast to the rational advancement of people and society promoted at Waterloo, the Gardens suggested something altogether more emotionally charged.

The Festival's main sites were orchestrated so as to provide a narrative-led experience that was at once celebratory, educational and fun. The story of national development through ingenuity, effort and technology was aligned with that of personal emancipation. The individual and the collective were presented as mutually supporting entities rather than as the opposing forces that they now represent.

The cultural alignments implicit in the Festival environment began to be seriously revised during the 1970s. Rayner Banham, writing in 1976, condemned the Festival as representing a cultural and architectural cul-de-sac. Now, and after 30 more years of critical equivocation, these Festival alignments appear more attractive than ever.

1. Hillier, 1976, 26
2. Margaret Garlake (1998) has examined the extraordinary artistic energy of the Festival in relation to the cultural politics of post-war reconstruction and international re-alignments. She places the Festival in relation to longer-term considerations of patronage and prestige. Not surprisingly, the Festival is marked down, despite its energy, for being so ephemeral a project.
3. Manser, 2000, 120.
4. Curtis, 1985.
5. Games, Moriarty and Rose, 2003, 75.
6. Games, Moriarty and Rose, 2003.
7. Games, Moriarty and Rose, 2003, 78.
8. Bailey bridges are pre-engineered, made in ready-to-assemble components and had been successfully used by the military during the war.
9. The architectural development of the Festival Hall is well documented; Clough Williams-Ellis (1951) provides a detailed history of the project and its genesis from idea to realisation.
10. Cox, 1951, 41-62.
11. Punch, 1951, lxxi.
12. Conekin, 2003, 94-100.
13. Lewis, 1994, 143-4.
14. Hopkinson, 1941.
15. Orwell, 1941.
16. Abercrombie, 1945.
17. Dunnett, 1951, 7.
18. Baron, 1951.

Catalogue for the Exhibition of Sculpture at Battersea

ART AND DEMOCRACY AT THE FESTIVAL

The new architecture of the Festival promoted the structures of the nascent social democracy in Britain. The schools, health centres and public buildings of this new Britain were Modernist in style and, by their defining logic, utilitarian and functionalist. It was important, in these circumstances of renewal, that the decoration of these buildings and spaces should be egalitarian, democratic and progressive. Accordingly, the open spaces of the Festival were dotted with large-scale sculptures. These broke with historical precedent and eschewed the usual subjects of public sculpture: kings, queens and generals.

Sculpture

The attempt to extend the potential range of public sculpture was broadly successful. The Festival launched a generation of British sculptors onto an international stage. Notwithstanding the evident success of this project over the long term (think of Epstein, Hepworth and Moore along with the more recent Gormley, Kapoor and Whiteread) it is worth considering how problematic the public display of sculpture remains. The present day discussions over the plinth in Trafalgar Square remind us that issues of taste and cost are always ready to undo these public gains.

In addition to the sculptural big-hitters of Moore, Epstein and Hepworth, the selection of artists and work was relatively cautious. From our own perspective the names of Reg Butler, Lynn Chadwick, Eduardo Paolozzi and Victor Passmore stand out as recognisable.[1]

Hugh Casson recalls that the Festival Design Group made the choice of sculptors for the South Bank.[2] The intention had been for the architects to suggest suitable work. Casson considers that the system was fatally compromised by the group's seeming inability to get beyond the name of Henry Moore.

In fact, the politics of commission were somewhat more complicated than Casson suggests. The Festival organisers and the Arts Council had become involved in an unintended rivalry. The Arts Council took the view that the Festival objectives and the brevity of the Festival project placed the South Bank beyond their normal priorities. Furthermore, they considered their stewardship of the better-known artists to be propriatorial. Accordingly, the Arts Council organised its own exhibition of Sculpture in Battersea Park.[3] Even there, the displays were compromised by the Council's use of a two-tier system that effectively promoted the already successful artists ahead of their more junior colleagues.

In the end, the Festival failed in its ambition to promote sculptural commission to a wider audience beyond the capital. Those ambitions were only realised, some 50 years later, by the success of Lottery funding in promoting the more diverse and widespread use of visual art in public spaces.

The sculptors and artists themselves contributed to the problem by conducting their Festival post-mortem within the context of a series of debates held at the Institute of Contemporary Arts in London during 1952.[4] The unashamedly elitist nature of this institution was matched only by its utter inability to project the significance of its functions to anyone beyond its own membership.

Coincidentally, the *Architectural Review* began to promote the wider use of sculpture within the urban environments of 'Townscape' just as the Festival was opening. With the exception of Harlow New Town, which seems to have embraced this idea enthusiastically, most local councils took a more pragmatic view and followed the *Review's* suggestion in thinking of street furniture as sculptural entities in 'Townscape' planning.

Indicative list of public sculpture on the South Bank:

Reg Butler, *Birdcage*

Lynn Chadwick Copper, *Abstract, Cypress*

S Charoux, *The Islanders*

Mitzi Cunliffe, *Root Bodied Forth*

Frank Dobson, *London Pride*

Georg Ehrlich, *Head of a Cow, Sick Boy*

Jacob Epstein, *Youth Advances*

Keith Godwin, *Neptune*

Dora Gordine, *Dyak*

Daphne Hardy Henrion, *Youth*

Heinz Henghes, *Orpheus*

Barbara Hepworth, *Contrapuntal Forms, Dynamic Forms*

R Huws Water, *Mobile Fountain*

Karin Jonzen, *A Dancer Begins*

Maurice Lambert, *Fish*

David McFall, *Boy and Foal*

F E McWilliam, *Spring*

Anna Mahler, *Woman with Pitcher*

John Matthews, *The Sisters, Grace*

Henry Moore, *Reclining Figure*

Victor Pasmore, *Shallow Relief Mural*

Eduardo Paolozzi, *Wall Fountain*

Peter Peri, *Sunbathers*

Karel Vogel, *The Industries*

Edward Wright, *Wood Mobile*

Mural Paintings on the South Bank

Another important element in the visual identity of the Festival was the widespread use of mural decoration to embellish the public spaces and façades of the buildings. Many exhibitions also included the use of mural elements as didactic and decorative elements in the storytelling of the Festival.

The painted mural was a spectacular legacy of the 1930s when artists such as Ravilious, Bawden, and Rex Whistler each experimented with the form to produce large-scale work within the context of modern architecture and decoration.

The rediscovery of the mural is linked to the steel-frame construction of modernist buildings. Removing the load bearing, or structural function of walls opened up much larger spaces within such buildings. In North America, the use of murals on buildings had been embraced by corporate capitalism. The *New Deal's* Works Progress Administration for public buildings also made widespread use of the mural. Ironically, the most famous muralists in North America were the Mexican revolutionaries: Diego Rivera, David Siqueiros and Jose Orozco.

It was natural, therefore, that as the architecture of welfare and public provision developed in Britain after 1945, and as exemplified by the Festival, efforts should be made to find appropriate forms of decoration for these new types of building. The potential of the mural was evident from its success in North America and, to a certain extent, within the Socialist Realist context of the USSR.

Some use of the mural had been made during WWII in Britain. Kenneth Rowntree, a pacifist and Quaker, passed some of the war painting large mural decorations for the British Restaurants where service personnel and workers could be assured of hot food and drink on a 24-hour basis. It was Rowntree who painted a mural depicting aspects of British History for the Lion and Unicorn Pavillion.

Ascher, the British textile company, experimented with the possibilities of screen-printing large linen panels for similar purposes and with the advantage of series production. This proved difficult with very few workshops able to provide the expertise to work to such a large scale. Only four panels were produced and in very limited number: two by Matisse and two by Henry Moore.

The range of artists employed on murals was quite extensive and included heavyweights, such as Ben Nicholson and Graham Sutherland, whose work was designed to survive beyond the natural limits of the Festival. There were artists from the politically-active Artists' International, James Boswell and James Fitton, along with a larger group broadly sympathetic to the social democratic ambitions of the Festival: John Armstrong, Edward Bawden, Tristram Hillier, John Hutton, Feliks Topolski, Julian Trevelyan and Mary Fedden. Newer artists such as John Minton and Keith Vaughan were also commissioned.

The scale of the mural schemes required the work of assistants on several of them. This part of the project therefore sustained a large community of artists.

Major painted murals displayed at the Festival and their locations[5]

John Armstrong *mural* for telecinema

John Barker *ground floor mural* in the Television pavilion

Edward Bawden *Country Life* in the Lion and Unicorn pavilion

Peter Bender *exterior mural* for Television pavilion

James Boswell *Drifters* in the Sea and Ships display

KC Chapman *River* in the Land display

Bernard Cheese *Kaleidoscope* in the 1851 pavilion

Jesse Collins *Paint Industry* in Power and Production display

J Dernbach *Mosaic* in the Earth display

Fred Excell *Surveyors* in the Land display

Pearl Falconer *Nursery Section* in Homes and Gardens

Mary Fedden *first floor mural* in the Television pavilion

Patricia Field *Fisheries* in Sea and Ships display

James Fitton *Introduction* in Homes and Gardens

 Seaside Features in Seaside display

Carl Giles *Seaside Family* in Seaside display

Edward Bawden's preliminary watercolour study for the British Character & Tradition mural for the Royal College of Art's Lion and Unicorn Pavilion

Walter Greave *Design Review* in the Design Review display
Kathleen Hale *Nursery* in New Schools display
Josef Herman *Mural of Miners* in Minerals of the Island display
Tristram Hillier *Propulsion* in the Sea and Ships display
Lewitt Him *New Schools* in New Schools display
Denys Hinton *ground floor mural* in the Television pavilion
Leonard Horton *The Beginnings of Science* in the Physical World display
James Hull *Chemical Products* in the Physical World display
    Crystal Forms in the Physical World display
John Hutton *exterior mural* for the Sea and Ships display
Barbara Jones *Coastline* in the Seaside display
    first floor mural in the Television pavilion
Kempster and Evans *Research at Sea* in the Sea display
Augustud Lunn *Glass Paintings* in the Seaside display
John Minton *Exploration* in the Dome of Discovery
Charles Mozley *Florence Nightingale* in the Health display
Ben Nicholson *interior mural* for the Thameside Restaurant
Victor Pasmore *external mural* for the Regatta Restaurant
John Piper *exterior mural — the English Man's Home* for the Homes and
    Garden pavilion
Hilda Pope *Zones of Life* in the Sea display
Brian Robb *Parlours* in Homes and Gradens
Robert Scanlan *No Man's Land and Invasions*, both for the People of
    Britain display
Laurence Scrafe *Nuclear Physics* in the Physical World display
    external mural for the Regatta Restaurant
George Skolly *Shipbuilding* for the Sea and Ships display
Graham Sutherland *Landscape* in the Land of Britain display
Lyn Thompson *Power and Production* in the Power and Production display
Feliks Topolski *Empire* under the arches
John Tunnard *interior mural* in the Regatta Restaurant
Keith Vaughan *Discovery* in the Dome of Discovery

1. David Burstow (Harwood and Powers, 2001, 95) has described the sculpture of the South Bank in detail.
2. Harwood and Powers, 2001, 97.
3. Garlake, 1998, 217.
4. Harwood and Powers, 2001, 102.
5. List compiled from *Catalogue of Exhibits* (HMSO 1951).

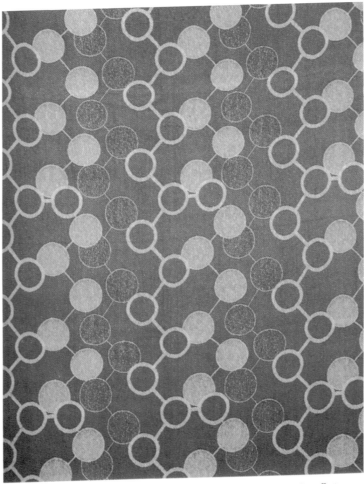

Festival Textile fabric using atomic and molecular forms to decorative effect

PATTERN AND SCIENCE AT THE FESTIVAL

Throughout the Festival there was a complementary and consistent allusion to the utopian possibilities afforded by the scientific and technological determinants of modern Britain.

The Festival Pattern Group enhanced the scientific projection that was integral to the Festival's objectives. This project began in 1949 with the presentation of a paper by Kathleen Lonsdale to the Society of Industrial Arts. The subject of the paper was crystallography and one of its points was that crystal patterns were suitable for contemporary textiles.

The pottery manufacturer Midwinter produced a range of contemporary ceramics, with designs by Hugh Casson, Terrence Conran and Jessie Tate, which effectively promoted the Festival ethos as 'lifestyle'. The designs on this pottery are suggestive of the themes promoted by the Pattern Group.

In the end, almost half the schemes promoted in collaboration with the Festival Pattern Group were for textiles. This reflected two significant facts: first, the obvious importance of the textile industry within Britain's manufacturing sector at that time; second, that, coincidentally, the Chairman of the Council of Industrial Design (CoID) at the end of the 1940s was Sir Thomas Barlow, owner of Barlow and Jones, a major cotton manufacturer.

The participation of the CoID means that the activities of the pattern Group are well documented. It is, therefore, possible to identify the designers and makers of specific fabric designs associated with the Festival in a way that is not always the case. Schoeser describes project in detail.[1]

The most significant contribution of the Pattern group to the Festival was the decoration of the Regatta Restaurant designed by

Misha Black. The restaurant, which faced the river, commanded spectacular views towards Whitehall. Another major feature of the Regatta Restaurant was the *Surrey* pattern drapes by Marianne Straub.

The concept of using crystal and molecular forms in decoration was, in 1951, a recent one. The technical possibilities of microscopy, the branch of photography associated with the very large magnification of very small objects, had only recently developed a sufficient capability.

The scientific projection at the Festival was comprised of several elements. The scientific displays were integral to the main narrative of the Festival. The Dome of Discovery, the Shot Tower, the Skylon, and the Power and Production Pavilion could all claim to be scientific exhibits that wove contemporary scientific achievements into a historical narrative, beginning with Newton and continuing through the agrarian and industrial revolutions to the present.

This narrative of historical development came to a powerful climax with the mythology of a crucial scientific and technological contribution to the successful prosecution of WWII. This myth was evidenced by Britain's status as an atomic power and the technological leads that it had in such fields as radar, computers, tele-communications, television and jet engines. The Festival sought to project this successful narrative into the future through establishing a lexicon of pattern based on molecular and crystal shapes. The resulting association of scientific rationalism and decoration was entirely suited to the Festival's modernist promotion of technical education.

The obvious parallel between molecular structures and modular systems in modern engineering and architecture was emphasised by the construction of several connecting screens across the South Bank site.

In addition to the South Bank, there was an important scientific exhibition at the Science Museum. This more permanent exhibit and the extension to the museum was testimony to the longer-term significance of scientific education to national prosperity.

A feature of the South Kensington exhibit was the association of scientific observation with the idea of discovery and adventure.

This theme was established in the opening rooms of the exhibit that featured an *Alice in Wonderland* inversion of scale effects. A proposal for a 'Newton-Einstein House', which subjected visitors to extreme gravitational forces, was ultimately rejected.[2]

The scientific adventure of discovery was, therefore, identified with the excitement and extremes of fairground rides. Thus, the coherence of the Festival experience was established across all its sites, including Battersea.

The activities of the Pattern Group and the widespread use of molecular, crystal and other scientific imagery within the visual rhetoric of the Festival were greatly enhanced by the technical association with photography. In the public imagination, photography was intuitively accorded the status of objective evidence.

This was especially the case in relation to scientific issues where very small objects were not normally visible. So, the Pattern Group's projects further revealed a reality normally hidden from view. The very presence of these decorations carried with it an implicit acknowledgement of Britain's technical genius. With hindsight, we can also understand that these photographic images also carried a suggestion of television. A suggestion made explicit elsewhere in the Festival Telecinema designed by Wells Coates.

The suggestive power of progress through science and technology became, through the effort of the Pattern Group, an important element in the Festival's vision of the future.[3] This vision, like that projected through the popular typographic styles of Festival lettering, was largely benign.

As an aside, it is worth reflecting that 1951 marked the publication of John Wyndham's *Day of the Triffids*. The narrative of scientific mutation and social catastrophe may be taken to mark the beginning of a growing scepticism and unease with regard to the progressive claims of scientific endeavour.

1. Harwood and Powers, 2001, 117
2. Forgan, 1998, 237
3. Conekin, 2003, 57

FESTIVAL TYPOGRAPHY AND PLEASURE

The design coherence of the South Bank was further promoted by the careful selection of particular typefaces for signage and information throughout the Festival.[1] Though the Typographic Committee gave minimal guidelines to typographers, designers and architects, it did seek to promote a typographic coherence across the whole Festival. The major consideration informing the Committee's approach was that the timbre of Festival lettering should be clearly differentiated from the ubiquitous sanserif faces of the 1930s and WWII. The Typographic Panel proposed that the lettering should be coherent without being uniform and should

WITH COMPLIMENTS

Festival of Britain 1951

SOUTH BANK EXHIBITION YORK ROAD LONDON SE1
WATERLOO 1951

Printed Festival compliment slip

obviously be informed by connection to English historical reference. Ideally, any such reference should be toward the popular and vernacular tradition.

Sanserif faces first appeared at the beginning of the 19th century, identified as 'grotesques'. Sanserif typefaces became widely used during the 1930s when the machine composition of Gill Sans had become the default typographic setting for contemporary and modern texts. The sanserif types had been further debased by use during WWII as the standard typeface of military imperative.[2]

Accordingly, the typographic identity of the Festival was constructed through the rediscovery of 18th century display types. These faces, called Fat, were distinguished by their slab and wedge serifs, low squat shapes and the relative weightiness of their imprint; the latter characteristic depending on the exaggerated emphasis accorded to their vertical elements, called stems, and resulting in their heightened visibility over distance.

This visibility made these faces ideal for the relatively specialised and limited use in shop fronts and early advertising notices. It is no co-incidence that these typefaces emerged at an historical moment associated with the development of market economies and seaside leisure resorts.

The resulting signage, underpinned by its historical references to English vernacular style, therefore helped orchestrate the Festival crowd to the happy rhythms of democratic diversity associated with market day and seaside holiday. These psychological and emotional associations went well beyond the limited potential of the purely functional tradition that had characterised the modern movement until then.

The Typographic Panel was made up of five members: Charles Hasler (Chair), Nicolette Gray, Gordon Cullen, Austin Frazer and Gordon Andrews. Cullen was in charge of external lettering and acted in an advisory capacity. The Panel published a sample book indicating the preferred direction in which it hoped to guide the designers and architects. The book presents an eclectic, but coherent, selection of Egyptian and Roman letters in condensed or extended forms and with shadows, blocks and outline variants. The sanserif form was allowed, but only in its early and eccentric 19th-century form.

Nikolaus Pevsner identified the guiding intelligence of the Typographic Panel as Gordon Cullen.[3] Pevsner and Cullen were colleagues at the *Architectural Review*, where both had contributed to the effort of trying to promote a specifically English resolution to the problems associated, at least in the cultural imagination, with the functional uniformity of Modernist systems. Pevsner, with his unimpeachably Continental and academic background was able to provide the theoretical framework for this project. Cullen was able to visualise this effort in terms of an architectural draughtsmanship organised by 'serial vision'.

In turn, this approach to looking at architectural environments was able to draw attention to the unfolding narratives of the experience of those environments. Cullen[4] described these experiential narratives by reference to the idea of 'townscape'. The varied environments, experiences and excitements of the South Bank anticipate this later codification.

The Typographic Panel also commissioned a two-dimensional shaded letterform, called *Festival Titling*, from Philip Boydell. The idea was "to give the impression of a third dimension without employing perspective or shadow effects". The resulting letter was able to allude to the cut-letter sharpness of classical tradition and, simultaneously, to the sanserif modern. The letter was a perfect complement to the fluttering dazzle effect of bunting that was a characteristic feature of all Festival sites.[5]

The Typographic Panel's loose directives were particularly useful in relation to the very large amount of printed material produced to promote and commemorate the Festival. The official publications set a standard for typographic design and clarity. The eclectic style favoured by the Panel was ideally suited to the constraints of the smaller provincial letterpress and chromo-litho printers employed to produce material at a local level. Many small pieces of Festival printing share the jaunty eclecticism of early 19th-century playbill design. This lucky association, derived from the material constraints of printers' stocks, exactly matched the wider objectives of the Typographic Panel.

Broadly speaking, the typographic identity of the Festival may be summarised as an attempt to recast recognisable elements of an English tradition in typographic design associated with popular pleasures and entertainments. This contemporary recasting repositioned the typographic traditions of village fête, market and seaside in contrasting relation to those of European Modernism (collective, authoritarian and undifferentiated) and associated them to a sign system for a developing economy increasingly identified as a leisure experience of material abundance and fun.

The success of the typographic project effectively created an allusive signage for the historical narratives of people and land around which the South Bank experience was constructed.

1. Rennie (Harwood and Powers 2001, 107) has described the typographic identity of the Festival in detail.
2. As an aside, it is worth noting that sanserif letterforms are not usually recommended for text composition. They are best used in the dramatic isolation of single words where their clear legibility communicates instruction quickly and with precision.
3. Penrose, 1952.
4. Cullen, 1961.
5. The dazzle effect is an important element in optical theory. During the 1950s it became increasingly used, to arresting effect, by fine artists and by advertising creative directors. Its first use was as an unexpected solution to the problem of camouflaging dreadnoughts during WWI. The technological advances that made dreadnought battleships possible altered the form of naval warfare. Ships would engage over large distances. In the absence of radar the service still relied on optical contact over great distance. It was obviously impossible to disguise the shape, size and bulk of these enormous naval structures. However, it was found that painting geometric forms on the ships made it very difficult over large distances to effectively estimate distance and direction.

Wedgwood mug

FESTIVAL SOUVENIRS

The official and unofficial souvenirs of the Festival take, as the images in this book demonstrate, a very wide range of forms. So far, I have tried to present the various contexts that explain why the Festival is important and why the experience of the Festival was so special for the people who took part in and visited the Festival.

Of course, the point about souvenirs is that they are objects with meanings beyond those normally associated with everyday concerns of functionality and value-for-money. The meanings of souvenirs rest in their associations with experience and feeling.

"The past is a foreign country", wrote L.P. Hartley in 1953. The timing of this observation could hardly have been more apt. By 1953, Britain had emerged from the catharsis of war and its attendant austerity and stood on the threshold of a new and dynamic future. The past, at least that part of it before WWII, could never have seemed more distant.

The idea, expressed by Hartley, suggests the literary potential of an engagement with history, memory and anthropology. In the 1930s, following WWI and its economic and political ramifications, this engagement had become practical. The immersion technique pioneered by George Orwell in *Down and Out* (1933) and *Wigan Pier* (1937) became the methodological foundation for Mass Observation.[1]

The social anthropologist Tom Harrisson's initial proposal was based on the notion that, in a highly stratified and class-based society such as Britain, the various demographic groups remained a mystery to each other. This was potentially catastrophic for the administrative elite, who – aware of a rising political consciousness across the wider demographics of women and the working class – remained unable to communicate effectively with a world they did not understand and with a people they could not comprehend.

The distance between the apparatus of government and the people it served through democracy had become especially problematic after 1918. The management of WWI became understood, with hindsight at least, to have been catastrophic, wasteful and duplicitous. The experience of the war provided a pretext for the post-war transformation of the franchise and social policy. This was an attempt by political interests, to accommodate a widespread and radicalised political consciousness that had been, itself, a consequence of the war. Economic events and political upheavals around the world and throughout the 1920s and '30s, confirmed the popular perception that the elite were no longer in control.

This trajectory of popular emancipation in Britain is marked by a series of international crises, most notably the Russian Revolution, the General Strike, the great crash and economic depression, the rise of Fascism and the Spanish Civil War. This backdrop of events, before WWII, provides the material for new writing as seen in J.B. Priestly's *English Journey* (1933) and George Orwell's *Down and Out*, *Wigan Pier* and *Homage to Catalonia* (1938). A similar evolution occured in visual culture, where *Picture Post* promoted a new photo-journalism by Bill Brandt and Bert Hardy, amongst others. It is into this matrix of popular and radical material that Mass Observation fits.

Harrisson proposed an intelligence-gathering investigation based on observation and volunteer reporters. The results were, notwithstanding their obvious subjectivity, compellingly vivid. The town of Bolton, Lancashire, was identified as 'Work Town' and became a detailed case study of life in the industrial working class.

Alongside Harrisson, Charles Madge and Humphrey Jennings were founding partners of Mass Observation. Madge was a journalist and poet closely allied with the British Surrealist movement. Jennings, also a poet and surrealist, is now remembered as a pioneer film documentarist of WWII. Madge and Jennings were, as might be expected of surrealists, interested in revealing or connecting to the subconscious characteristics of the various British tribes. The idea of the collective unconscious dominates many aspects of Mass Observation's work although it remains tantalizingly obscure.

The combination of anthropological organisation and surrealist methodology that distinguished Mass Observation was unique and provided a wealth of detailed and, to the administrative elite at least, surprising and valuable evidence. This was particularly valuable during the first eighteen months of WWII when it seemed, to Whitehall, that morale was at its most fragile.

However, the kinds of data provided by Mass Observation proved too complex for the interpretative machinery of government. Statistical polling methodologies evolved as an economic and more obviously scientific alternative to data management for government.

Against these trajectories and background, the Festival may be understood as an attempt to forestall any further radicalisation implicit in the social transformations of WWII through the projection of a benign social-democratic meritocracy. Ironically, those transformations played themselves out, during the 1960s, through the hedonistic and counter-cultural rejection of the disciplines associated with the previous ordering of society.

In contrast our engagement with the world of objects and material culture remains prosaic. The past is reconstructed through its objects. Our interactions with objects are usually described in relation to function, taste and perhaps aesthetics. Souvenirs generally score low against all of these markers. Accordingly, they have a marginal status and are not usually included in the narratives of taste officially sanctioned by the State.

The immediate circumstances of the Festival were determined by the relative economic and material constraints of austerity. Although not a trade fair, the Festival promoted an idea of the future configured around the potential of materials and technology to define a leisure economy. In 1951, this seemed as though it would be a simple extension of manufacturing technologies and efficiencies.

From that perspective, the permanent change that came to define the planned obsolescence of an affluent society, with its credit-based consumer culture, might as well have been from another planet.

To some extent that planet had already been glimpsed through the material abundance and affluence of the USA after WWII. It was no accident that artists such as Peter Blake became fascinated with the commercial and popular culture of North America. Peter Blake was a pioneer collector and curator of objects that were at once familiar and alien. The same possibility extends, today, for those of us interested in the early post-war period in Britain.

The most remarkable legacy of the Festival was, notwithstanding the subject of this book and the comments of this essay, its emotional timbre. Whatever the material difficulties of austerity, the Festival seems to have been enjoyed by its visitors. Given our contemporary anxieties of national identity and 'happiness economics', the Festival seems a likely source of clues as to how to reconcile affluence and anxiety.

The Festival souvenirs therefore remain significant in their meanings. This is, perhaps, surprising as these objects would not normally be considered worthy of study: they are inexpensive and, generally speaking, not particularly well made. By the criteria of design history or art history, so often obsessed with the iconic, they hardly exist.

The market in souvenir objects is long established. In their earliest relic forms, souvenirs were associated with religious pilgrimage.

By the 18th century, in Britain at least, the souvenir economy had evolved into a complex series of separate business, each aimed at a very specific class and taste. At the top end, the aristocratic grand tour supported an international trade in classical sculpture and works of art. At a more modest level there were souvenirs made to commemorate political struggle. These were clandestine objects that spoke of secular struggle and revolutionary sympathies.

Alternatively, during the 19th century and in sharp contrast to the radical values espoused through Enlightenment, there evolved a market in souvenirs that commemorated the enduring and constant presence of the monarchy in Britain.

Queen Victoria came to the throne in 1837. Her long reign, throughout the rest of the 19th century, gave expression to political stability and prosperity at home, manufacturing abundance and international military power. It was natural, in these circumstances, for the figure of Queen Victoria to become a powerful symbol across every class of population and for the myths of economic success, military power and intellectual superiority to cluster around this totem as the expression of Imperial destiny.

The mass market in commemorative souvenirs supported a range of manufacturers in every industry. From the end of the 19th century onwards, the prosperity associated with the productivity gains of industrial specialisation began to support a developing leisure economy. Souvenirs of day-trips and excursions were soon being produced to commemorate visits to the seaside and elsewhere.

By the end of the century, the picture postcard and photographic snapshot had become commonplace markers of sophistication, pleasure and class. The popular exchange of these artefacts evolved to celebrate the ties of community, friendship and family against a background of increasing social mobility.

It was appropriate, then, that the Festival exhibition of popular arts and traditions, *Black Eyes* and *Lemonade*, included a selection of souvenirs. These were grouped thematically into selections covering royal, martial, railway and seaside commemoratives, mementos and crested wares.[2]

It is interesting to note from the catalogue that many of the exhibits were drawn from the personal collections of Barbara Jones and Sir Arthur Elton (for the Crystal Palace and railway sections). The only institutional lender to the exhibition appears to be the Brighton Pavilion for those items relating to this fantastical seaside pavilion.

The conceptual sophistication implied by an interest in popular culture, folk art and souvenirs is evident from the limited number of lenders to the exhibition. The interest in the authentic, popular and everyday objects of rural past and industrial archaeology, implicit in the project, was not yet widespread. Indeed, it was actively discouraged through the formation of academic and refined taste.

Against the backdrop of this narrative, the souvenirs produced for the Festival have several unique characteristics. They are, for the most part, outside of the characteristic determinants of the market in Britain. They celebrate an idea of the secular state and citizenship that is at odds with the traditions of monarchy and the royal commemorative. Notwithstanding the obviously ideological nature of the Festival project, the souvenirs generally avoid too obvious a political association.

This is not so surprising when one considers that souvenirs have tended to be made by specialist manufacturers. The same firms that routinely made royal commemoratives and other such souvenirs produced these gently radical objects.

Robin Darwin reviewed a selection of souvenirs and listed a teapot stand made of heat resistant glass, a stud box, a tobacco box by the Metal Box Co Ltd, a horse brass by Max Gate Ltd of Birmingham, a compact by Evans Components, a slipper sock from Leicester, a toy and an 'optimistic' souvenir parasol.[3]

The keepsakes of 1951 may be divided into the officially sanctioned and the unofficial. A committee established through the Festival Office and the Council of Industrial Design selected the official souvenirs from the flood of proposals in the 18 months before the opening. Official souvenirs were allowed to carry the emblem of the Festival designed by Abram Games.

It is worth mentioning a small group of souvenirs that carry an unofficial version of the Festival emblem. This replaces Britannia with a masculine warrior figure and omits the drapes of bunting. These emblems, manufactured by Starferst (named after Mr. Ferst, the company's managing director), were cast in metal and the result is well enough made to be official looking, militaristic and intimidating. A variety of objects exist bearing this emblem: most are simply badges in a variety of sizes, but the grandest objects are a set of souvenir silver teaspoons.

The unofficial souvenirs constitute those overlooked by the Souvenir Committee or produced in parallel to these channels. Some were produced with an eye to the commercial main chance. Some were home made. Whatever their origins and status, it is noticeable that most of the Festival souvenirs are mass-produced and inexpensively priced. The democratic ambitions of the Festival were served in this respect at least.

One of the most charming characteristics of the smaller Festival celebrations is their implicit reference to county shows, village fêtes and garden parties. These events are commemorated by a multitude of ephemera ranging from printed guides to amateur snapshot photographs.

For those wishing to explore further afield, Collins published a series of regional travel guides edited by Geoffrey Grigson and labelled under the *About Britain* title; other contributors included

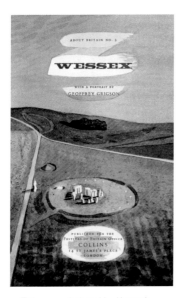

Title page, designed by Kenneth Rowntree

Title page, designed by E.W. Fenton

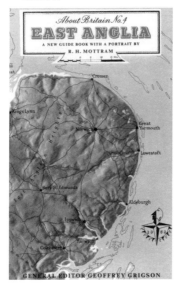

Geographical dust jacket and cover. The complete set made a map of Britain

Title page, designed by Barbara Jones

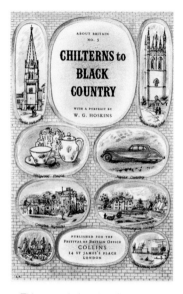

Title page, designed by S.R. Badmin

Title page, designed by Barbara Jones

Title page, designed by Kenneth Rowntree

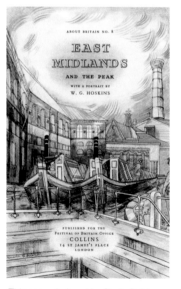

Title page, designed by Sheila Robinson

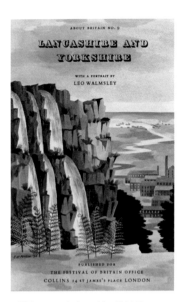

Title page, designed by E.W. Fenton

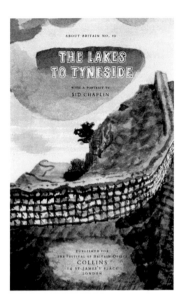

Title page, designed by Kenneth Rowntree

Title page, designed by John Worsley

Title page, designed by Joan Hassall

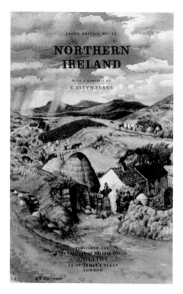

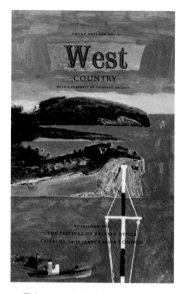

Title page, designed by S.R. Badmin

Title page, designed by Kenneth Rowntree

Leo Walmsley, R.H. Mottram and W.G. Hoskins. These guides were published by Collins as a joint venture with the Festival Office, and were sponsored by the Brewers' Society. They were intended to foster an exploration of the British regions and an enjoyment of their varied countryside.

In 1951, the English roadside and village public house was a staple of the rural community. Often, these public houses were historic and independent institutions. It was possible, in 1951, to travel the length and breadth of Britain using only public houses for board and lodging; following a long period of commercial consolidation and transformation, it would be almost impossible to do the same today.

The *About Britain* guides — notable for their pictorial title pages by Barbara Jones and Joan Hassall, and by S.R. Badmin, E.W. Fenton, Kenneth Rowntree and John Worsley — continued a tradition of illustrated guides that had begun with John Betjeman's *Shell County Guides* prior to WWII.

These books provide, along with various other guides published after WWII, for the more widespread adoption of a neo-romantic sensibility. This project had been furthered, during WWII, by the *Recording Britain* scheme, to which the majority of the above mentioned artists contributed. The *About Britain* guides were remarkable for the inclusion of colour photographs when these were still unusual in popular and inexpensive books.

The GPO issued a commemorative stamp for the Festival and *Cinderella labels* (non-postage stamps) for envelopes were produced as London souvenirs.

Generally speaking, Festival souvenirs have several levels of interest to contemporary collectors. The first is that the Festival was spectacularly ephemeral. The immediate destruction of Festival's physical environment effectively drew a line under the project. So, the souvenirs associated with the Festival speak of something that has literally disappeared from view.

So, the souvenirs have a special and unique status. They provide evidence of something that has disappeared and that we can no longer imagine. In this context, the souvenirs can be understood as the archaeological remains of another world. Peculiarly, that world, because of the Festival's ideological purpose, is about both the past and the future. In consequence, the archaeological reconstruction of the Festival experience, through its souvenirs, is defined as both science fiction and nostalgia.

Clearly, the extent and scope of the Festival make any definitive collection impossible. There are simply too many official and unofficial items. However, important documentary collections have been built up by the Museum of London and by Sheffield Hallam University.

The political and collecting economies of the Festival collide in unexpected ways. Some items, such as the *Official Guide to the South*

Bank, survive in quantity. Other items – such as the Skylon pen and holder, and the black-and-white Wedgwood mug – survive in much smaller quantities. The short production runs of post-war Britain may explain this. By our own contemporary standards, the retail market and the souvenir economy of 1951 were tiny and fragmented. In addition many of the items produced were ephemeral. That they have survived at all is miraculous.

As a result of the themes, which determined the scope and ambitions of the Festival project, and because of its particular historical moment, the Festival speaks simultaneously of the future and the past. This is relatively unusual. The 'white heat' of the 1960s and the social transformations of meritocracy in Britain appeared to have reduced the symbolic power of our institutions.

The unlikely possibility of combining the future and the past has made the sort of collecting described here especially interesting to modern artists. The re-discovery of utopia through an archaeological reinvention of the past is a characteristic of the conceptual art of the 1990s. The works of the Chapman Brothers, Jeremy Deller, Mark Dion and Grayson Perry amongst others, each explore the constructive potential of everyday objects.

1. The full literary and ideological potential of these approaches is documented by Benedict Anderson (1983) and expressed in his idea of 'imagined community'.

2. Jones, 1951, 34-36.
3. CoID, 1951, 55.

POSTSCRIPT – THE IDEA OF THE FESTIVAL

The Festival occurred at a decisive moment in mass culture. It was the last event to be produced in a cultural landscape not dominated by television.

It is interesting to contrast the Festival with Queen Elizabeth II's Coronation in 1953. The latter event was used to introduce live television as a mass-communication phenomenon. So, the Festival predates the widespread experience of television. Moving images of the Festival, so significant in our contemporary construction of popular history, are accordingly rare.

The televisual legacy of the Coronation, on the other hand, is recognised as culturally significant in terms of national identity, monarchy and television history. These images are re-visited, at regular intervals, through the celebratory prisms of jubilee and anniversary.

Peculiarly, the Festival was almost immediately unfashionable amongst the cultural commentators of the Establishment class who attached the Festival, after 1951, to an agenda of national decline. Now, after fifty years, the Festival and South Bank are beginning to appeal to new generations unencumbered by post-war resentments.

Any investigation of the Festival begins with a reading of two key texts: Michael Frayn's essay 'Festival' in *The Age of Austerity*,[1] and Reyner Banham's essay in *A Tonic to the Nation*.[2]

Frayn's essay accounts for the Festival in relation to the class interests of its "herbivore" protagonists. These interests are contrasted with those of the rapacious "carnivore" class who, not surprisingly, are presented as dominant. Their project of attacking Festival values and replacing them with an atomised, consumerist

Colour art-print of the South Bank, signed Herbert J. Williams

alternative is regretfully acknowledged as the inevitable
consequence of a crude and philistine, but powerful, intelligence
cast in Darwinist terms.

From this perspective, even in 1964, the Festival was already
disappearing. In fact, Festival values lingered a good while longer. For
Banham, the middle class interests identified by Frayn were, however
well intentioned and radical, part of a characteristic loss of nerve.
Something stronger had been required and was still needed. Banham's
analysis, published to coincide with the 25th anniversary of the
Festival, established the main characteristics of the Festival style as
effete and whimsical, inward looking and, by implication, provincial.

Banham's cultural critique of the post-war settlement, implicit in
his promotion of a convenient and hedonistic consumer society, is
a criticism of an intellectual austerity associated with high culture
and the industrial disciplines of old-fashioned factory production.

Banham's position may be understood by reference to the market ideologies that had emerged during the early 1970s as an attempt to dismantle the post-war settlement.

The fortunes of the South Bank have mirrored the wider picture of decline that characterised, at least until recently, the received view of British post-war history. Generally, the narratives of national decline have been presented through loss of great power status, catastrophic economic weakness and of unsustainable welfare provision (the over-reaching State). These perceptions have, inevitably and along with the regular help of political scandal, increased public cynicism towards the political elite.

Correlli Barnett's histories, published as the *Pride and Fall* sequence (from 1972 onwards), have established the declinist case by explaining Britain's loss of great-power status as a consequence of social transformations set in train by the experience of the Second World War. Placing the military victories of WW2 in contrast with the lost opportunities of post-war reform and social democracy helped establish a revisionist political agenda for the 1980s. Neither Penny Sparke[3] nor Hillier and Banham[4] convincingly disabuse this tendency.

The historical trajectory proposed by Barnett opposed that put forward by Angus Calder.[5] This identified the popular experience of the Second World War, as recorded through Mass Observation, as a consciousness-raising, emancipatory and liberating phenomenon. Calder thereby explained the Labour victory of 1945 as a political consequence of the social transformations unleashed by the shared experiences of WWII.

In fact, Calder's historical analysis substantiates Orwell's hypothesis that the demands of WWII would irrevocably transform British society.[6] At its strongest, Orwell's argument proposes these social transformations as both revolutionary and as a necessary condition for victory. Orwell and Calder's historical trajectory of social revolution has been called into question constantly, most recently by Sonya Rose.[7]

Dominic Sandbrook has questioned the emancipatory trajectory of popular cultural change during the 1950s and '60s.[8] Although the Festival is beyond the immediate scope of Sandbrook's writing, the implication is that the Festival, and everything it stood for, was part of a "lost" period of the early 1950s.

It should be noted, again, that no such anxiety attaches itself to the other popular festival of the early 1950s: the Coronation of 1953. Peter Hennessy describes how the Coronation celebrations played well to American television audiences and this, in turn, established a significance for those images beyond their obvious meanings in relation to monarchy, tradition and ceremony.[9] So, the images of the Coronation were important for a nascent television industry and also as part of a political project to reclaim some cultural capital in the face of American economic superiority.

These revisions, intentionally or not, each further diminish the cultural legacy of meritocratic social democracy established after WWII. The Festival of Britain is, accordingly, written out of this historiography. Even Hennessy, whose political history is sympathetic to the idealistic aims of reform, gives the Festival short shrift.[10] Peculiarly, the Festival falls almost exactly between the two periods he has, so far, chosen to examine.

Of course, these kinds of histories draw on the official records and memoranda of an establishment elite. They are about the histories of power and influence. In the context of these histories, it has proved difficult to place the Festival and its values accurately as evidence of popular feeling.

The popular success of the Festival and the enduring popularity of the Festival Hall as concert venue and meeting place have conspired to confound this critical and Establishment equivocation around the South Bank. Like the cathedral at Coventry, the Festival Hall has been embraced for its meanings and symbolism as much as for the success of its design.

All of these phenomena have conspired to separate the remaining traces of the Festival from the utopian meanings attached to them at the time. The souvenirs of the Festival, mixed in quality as they are, provide an important reminder to the popular experience of 1951.

These souvenirs provide for a sort of archaeology of 1951. The objects speak of both the past and the future. The past comprises the culture and traditions celebrated by the Festival in 1951. We can, if we visited the Festival, recall this and feel nostalgic. It is important to acknowledge that the popular memory of the Festival, as evidenced through recollection, is entirely positive: no-one, it seems, recalls the Festival with disappointment!

The Festival also promised the possibility of a post-war reconstruction that redefined British society in terms of democracy, education and opportunity. The utopia anticipated by the Festival would be in a state of continuous improvement supported by developments in technology and engineering. The future of Britain was imagined as rational, modernist and social-democratic.

Obviously, this particular future has not worked out exactly as planned. Nevertheless, the souvenirs of the Festival have some of this anticipatory energy by association. In consequence, they speak of an alternative future that might have been and constitute a kind of science fiction.

From where we are now, the Festival has not simply disappeared it has become rationally inconceivable. In consequence, the Festival has become literally invisible.

Perhaps because of the experimental and utopian legacy of the Festival, the South Bank became identified as a problem site. By the 1980s its concrete 'brutalist' landmarks of the 1960s and '70s had become unfashionable. The South Bank's avant-gardist cultural programming was, at least during the 1970s, as alienating to the general public as the absence of adequate street lighting. The unsolicited use of the South Bank as shelter and skate-park diminished its reputation further.

The recent problems of the South Bank have attracted various architectural solutions. These have usually involved erasing the remaining Festival legacy and re-casting the site through the enclosure, or franchising, of the remaining public spaces.

In contrast, the current redevelopment of the Festival Hall combines a sensitive architectural enhancement with the provision of modern leisure and retail facilities on the river frontage, whilst retaining the important open-air aspects of the riverside.

The work of Cedric Price during the 1960s developed various themes of the Festival architecture along bigger and more versatile lines. Price conceived of a large-scale commercial architecture of mega-structures whose interiors could be adapted to suit a variety of purposes.

Price's ideas were taken up by the architectural avant-gardists Archigram and provide the basis for the Pompidou centre's large open-plan spaces, designed by Richard Rogers and Renxo Piano, and engineered by Peter Rice.

Peter Rice later created a temporary inflatable structure for the South Bank[11] with Future Systems. This, along with the London Eye, has confirmed the South Bank's status, from 1951 onwards, as an ongoing architectural laboratory.

The present refurbishment of the South Bank has cleverly plugged itself into the urban renaissance of London. The South Bank now provides an access point, along with Borough and Tate Modern, to a revitalised and metropolitan hinterland from Waterloo, inland, to the Elephant and Castle.

1. Sissons and French, 1964, 330-352.
2. Banham and Hillier, 1976, 190.
3. Sparke, 1986.
4. Hillier and Banham, 1976.
5. Calder, 1969.
6. Orwell, 1941.

7. Rose, 2003.
8. Sandbrook, 2005 and 2006.
9. Hennessy, 2006, 245.
10. Hennessy, 1992 and 2006.
11. Rice, 1994, 9.

RIBA pamphlet with proposals for reconstruction, c.1944. From 1941 onwards, reconstruction and social planning were acknowledged in Britain as legitimate war aims. A huge publishing endeavour supported the debate around these issues

County of London Plan, Penguin, 1945. A shorter and simpler presentation of Professor Patrick Abercrombie's proposals for post-war reconstruction, development and environmental conservation

Souvenir jigsaw of Festival opening ceremony at St Paul's cathedral

Greetings card with bird's-eye view of the South Bank

Souvenir Micromodel paper building kit of the South Bank

Special Festival issue of *The Tatler* magazine

The emblem re-drawn by Fougasse
(Kenneth Bird) for *Punch*

GPO postage stamps commemorating the Festival

Tobacco tin manufactured by the Metal Box Company

Souvenir embossed card label

Festival soap by Wheen, London

Plastic souvenir badge

Festival photograph: the Skylon

Magazine advertisement for souvenir Skylon ballpoint pen and holder

Front of visitor plan
for the South Bank

Micromodel paper building
kit of the Skylon

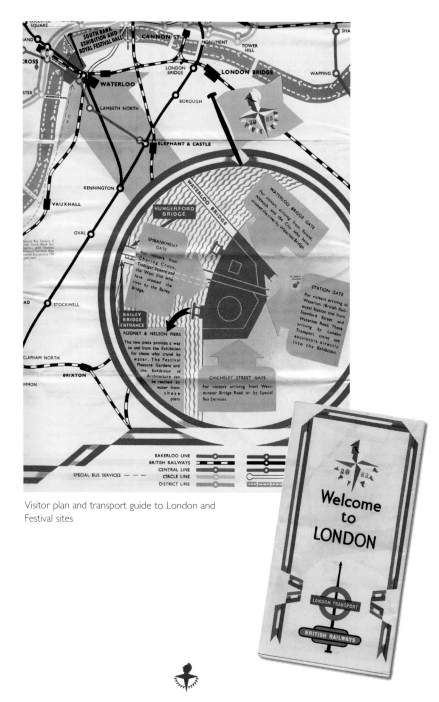

Visitor plan and transport guide to London and
Festival sites

Antelope outdoor metal chair, designed by Ernest Race

661 dining chair by Robin Day, for use in the restaurant at the Royal Festival Hall. An armchair version of this design was also produced

Antelope outdoor metal bench, designed by Ernest Race

Outdoor metal chair, designed by Robin Day

South Bank snapshot: Antelopes overlooking the Dome of Discovery

South Bank snapshot: resting on Antelopes

Souvenir programme for *Mister Sachs's Song Saloon*. Battersea. This show was a forerunner of the famous TV music-hall revival compered by Leonard Sachs. The cover features an amusing cut-out moustache so as to create a period feel amongst the 1951 audience.

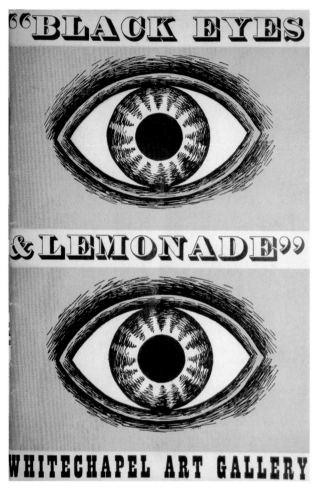

Catalogue cover for the *Black Eyes and Lemonade* exhibition of Folk art at the Whitechapel Art Gallery

Humber Cycle Girl Beauty Pageant poster

Poster for the Exibition of Science, South Kensington, designed by Robin Day

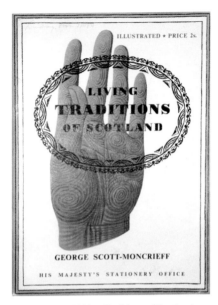

Arts Council Living Traditions of Scotland exhibition

Special souvenir of Norwich festivities

Needlework pictorial map. The pattern for this map was distributed in the press, so the souvenir could then be stitched at home

Festival Textile fabric using atomic and molecular forms to decorative effect

Transport Information poster, published by London Transport and
designed by Abram Games

Jigsaw of the South Bank

Jigsaw of the South Bank presented by Sharp's Toffee

Festival poster designed by
Abram Games

The Listener BBC magazine,
special Festival issue

Festival book design – *The Little Red Engine Goes to Town* by
Diana Ross

South Bank snapshot: John Cobb's Railton car, the holder of the World's Landspeed Record (exhibit G500), under the Dome of Discovery

South Bank snapshot: sculpture and open spaces

Opposite. South Bank snapshot medley: Skylon and about

Photograph of the Festival riverside, showing the shot-tower

South Bank snapshot: the riverside viewing platforms

Festival snapshot: the Royal Festival Hall

Festival snapshot: the riverside from Westminster Bridge

(This page and opposite) Festival Postcards

SEASIDE   South Bank Exhibition   Festival of Britain 1951

INTERIOR POWER AND PRODUCTION PAVILION   South Bank Exhibition   Festival of Britain 1951

ROYAL FESTIVAL HALL—FLOODLIT

FAIRWAY FOUNTAINS AND TRANSPORT PAVILION   South Bank Exhibition   Festival of Britain 1951

Festival postcard: the Fairway fountains and Transport pavilion

Souvenir 'Cinderella' stamp
of the Dome of Discovery

Souvenir 'Cinderella'
stamp of the South Bank

SPORTS ARENA   South Bank Exhibition   Festival of Britain 1951

Festival postcard: the Sports arena (beneath the Shot Tower)

Souvenir 'Cinderella' stamp
with Travelling Land exhibit

Souvenir 'Cinderella' stamp
with Festival Ship *Campania*

Festival postcard: the Guinness Clock at Battersea designed by
Lewitt Him (Jan Lewitt and George Him)

GUINNESS IN FESTIVAL LAND

The Walrus and the Carpenter
    Were walking hand in hand;
They strolled across the River Thames
    From half way down the Strand.
" *I think*," declared the Carpenter,
    " *This Festival is grand!* "

They marvelled at a thousand things
    Upon the South Bank Site:
They sent a message to the moon
    At twice the speed of light.
" *I hope*," remarked the Carpenter,
    " *The moon can read and write.* "

The Pleasure Gardens gave them both
    An afternoon of fun;
The Walrus grew a trifle warm
    From sporting in the sun.
" *I too*," confessed the Carpenter,
    " *Am feeling rather done.* "

They watched the Guinness Clock, and saw
    The minutes hurry past:
" *The time has come*," the Walrus said
    " *—I hope it isn't fast.* "
" *Not likely*," said the Carpenter,
    " *It's Guinness Time at last.* "

HAVE A GUINNESS WHEN YOU'RE TIRED
    G.E.11

Colour advertisement: The Guinness Clock, Battersea

THE DANCE PAVILION, FESTIVAL PLEASURE GARDENS, BATTERSEA.

Tote bag with
Festival fabric,
courtesy FOB Soc

Printed tin-plate souvenir
money box with Shot Tower

Festival pennants in printed felt

Coloured Wedgwood Mug

Paragon souvenir mug, courtesy
FOB Soc

Bretby pottery mug

Festival Toby, courtesy FOB Soc

Plastic Souvenir tumbler

Staffordshire pottery mug

Staffordshire box and cover, marked
'Bournemouth and Poole'

Painted Poole Pottery plate

Metal tea-pot

Festival souvenir medal

Festival souvenir medal

Festival Crown

Woven manufacturer's lablel

Printed paper napkin

Souvenir scarf from the
Festival of Britain

Souvenir scarf from the
Festival of Britain

London souvenir scarf with Festival emblem

Festival of Britain souvenir picture scarf of the South Bank

Souvenir headscarf with Lion and Unicorn, designed by James Gardner for Ascher, London

Child's party dress in Festival fabric

Visitor guide to
London and the
Festival

BIBLIOGRAPHY

Festival Guides

Baron, S., (1951), *FOB Pleasure Gardens Guide*, London, Festival Gardens Ltd

Baron, S., (1951), *FOB Souvenir in Pictures London*, News Chronicle

Bronowski, J., (1951), *Exhibition of Science London*, HMSO

Cox, I., (1951), *The South Bank Exhibition*, London, HMSO

Cox, I., (1951), *Festival Ship Campania*, London, HMSO

Dunnett, H. McG., (1951), *Exhibition of Architecture, Town Planning and Building Research*, London, HMSO

FOB, (1951), *Catalogue of Exhibits*, London, HMSO

FOB, (1951), *Land Travelling Exhibition*, London, HMSO

HMSO, (1951), *The Official Book of the Festival of Britain*, London, HMSO

Jones, B., (1951), *Black Eyes and Lemonade*, London, Whitechapel Art gallery

LBC, (1951), *Festival of Britain Guide (Lambeth Edition)*, London

Punch, (1951), *The Festival Punch*, London, Bradbury Agnew & Co

General

Abercrombie, P., (1945), *Greater London Plan*, London, HMSO

Anderson, B., (1983), *Imagined Community*, London, Verso

Appleyard, B. (1989), *The Pleasures of Peace*, London, Faber

Banham, M. and Hillier, B., (1976), *A Tonic to the Nation*, London, Thames and Hudson

Barnett, C., (1995), *The Lost Victory*, London, Macmillan

Barbican, (1987), *A Paradise Lost*, London, BAG

Bard Graduate Center, (2005), *Wearing Propaganda*, London, Yale UP

CoID, (1947) *Design 1946*, London, HMSO

CoID, (1951), *Design in the Festival*, London, HMSO

CoID, (1951), *Suppliers of Industrial Exhibits*, London, CoID

Calder, A., (1991), *The Myth of the Blitz*, London, Pimlico

Campbell, L., (1996), *Coventry Catherdral*, Oxford, OUP

Conekin, B.E., (2003), *The Autobiography of a Nation*, Manchester, MUP

Colls, R., (2002), *Identity of England*, Oxford, OUP

Crosby, T., (1956), *This is Tomorrow*, London, Whitechapel Gallery

Cullen, G., (1961), *Townscape*, London, AP

Curtis, B., (1985), 'One Continuous Interwoven Story', *Block 11*, London, Middlesex Polytechnic

Design Museum, (1999), *Modern Britain 1929-1939*, London, DM

Fishenden, R.B., (1952), *Penrose Annual*, Leeds, Lund Humphries

Forgan, S., (1998), 'Festivals of Science and the Two Cultures', *British Journal of the History of Science*, Volume 31, 217-240

Frayn, M. (1964), 'Festival', *The Age of Austerity* (Sissons, M. and French, P.), London, Penguin, 330-352

Games, N., Moriarty, C. and Rose, J., (2003), *Abram Games*, London, Ashgate

Garlake, M., (1998), *New Art New World*, London, Yale

Gavin, O. and Lowe, A., (1985), 'Designing Desire', *Block 11*, London, Middlesex Polytechnic

Goldfinger, E., (1945), *The County of London Plan Explained*, London, Penguin

Gosling, D., (1996), *Gordon Cullen*, London, Academy

Harwood, E. and Powers, A., (2001), 'Festival of Britain', *Twentieth Century Architecture 5*, London, Twentieth Century Society (Rennie on Typography, Burstow on Sculpture and Schoeser on Textiles)

Hennessy, P., (1992), *Never Again*, London, Jonathan Cape

Hennessy, P., (2006), *Having It So Good*, London, Allen Lane

Hopkinson, T. (ed.), (1941), 'A Plan for Britain', *Picture Post*, London, Hulton

Ismay, H.L., (1960), *Memoirs of Lord Ismay*, London, Heinmann

Jackson, L., (2001), *Robin and Lucienne Day*, London, Mitchell Beazley

Jones, B., (1951), *The Unsophisticated Arts*, London, Architectural Press

Lewis, J., (1994), *Such Things Happen*, Stowmarket, Unicorn

Lewis, J. and Brinkley, J., (1954), *Graphic Design*, London, RKP

McCallum, I., (1951), *Modern Buildings in London*, London, Architectural Press

Manser, J., (2000), *Hugh Casson*, London, Viking

Miller, J., (2002), *Kenneth Rowntree*, London, Lund Humphries

Orwell, G., (1941), *The Lion and the Unicorn*, London, Searchlight

Orwell, G., (1947,) *The English People*, London, Collins

Packaard, V., (1960), *The Waste Makers*, London, Penguin

RIBA, (c.1944), *Planning for Reconstruction*, London, Architectural Press

RIBA, (c.1945), *Towards a New Britain*, London, Architectural Press

Rayner, G., (1997), *Austerity to Affluence*, London, Merrell Holberton

Rayner, G., Chamberlain, R. and Stapleton, A.M., (2003), *Artists' Textiles in Britain*, Woodbridge, Antique Collectors' Club

Rice, P., (1994), *An Engineer Imagines*, London, Ellipsis

Richards, J. and Pevsner, N., (1951), 'The South Bank', *The Architectural Review*, August 1951, London, Architectural Review

Rose, S.O., (2003), *Which People's War?*, Oxford, OUP

Ross, D. and Wood, L., (1952), *The Little Red Engine Goes to Town*, London, Faber

SoID, (1951), *Designers in Britain 3*, London, Allan Wingate

Sandbrook, D., (2005), *Never Had It So Good*, London, Little Brown

Sandbrook, D., (2006), *White Heat*, London, Little Brown

Sissons, M. and French, P., (1964), *The Age of Austerity*, London, Penguin

Sparke, P., (1986), *Did Britain Make It?*, London, Design Council

Tubbs, R., (1942), *Living in Cities*, London, Penguin

Special Festival bus ticket

Tubbs, R., (1945), *The Englishman Builds*, London, Penguin

Whiteley, N., (2002), *Reyner Banham*, Cambridge, MIT Press

Williams-Ellis, C., (1951), *The Royal Festival Hall*, London, Max
  Parrish and LCC

There are several short texts of related interest written by Paul
Rennie and published in *Antique Collecting*, the Antique Collectors'
Club magazine.

The Festival of Britain Society publishes a quarterly newsletter that
is packed with information, anecdotes and recollection.

ACKNOWLEDGMENTS

Festival village fête

My thanks to Karen, without whom this great adventure might never have started. I should also like to thank the friends and colleagues we've met along the way, including the members of the Festival Society and The 20th Century Society.